A Bouquet of Togetherness

In the garden bright and fair,
We gather blooms beyond compare.
Each petal holds a tale untold,
In colors vibrant, pure as gold.

With hands entwined, we share our dreams,
Like flowing rivers, gleaming streams.
Each fragrant breath, a bond we weave,
In every moment we believe.

Through gentle whispers, hearts align,
A tapestry of love, divine.
With every smile, we plant a seed,
In the soil of hope, we heed.

The sun will rise, and shadows fall,
Yet in our hearts, we hear the call.
To cherish every single day,
As petals drift and sway away.

So let us bloom, together strong,
In unity, where we belong.
A bouquet bright, of love's embrace,
Forever rooted in this space.

Harmony of Growth

In the garden, silence hums,
Roots entwine where life becomes.
Sunlight kisses each green leaf,
Nature's dance, our shared belief.

Tendrils stretch to meet the skies,
In harmony, our spirit flies.
Every season, lessons taught,
In growth, the unity we sought.

The Beauty of We

Together, we create a song,
In every note, where we belong.
With threads of kindness, hearts entwined,
A tapestry of souls combined.

Through laughter shared and tears we shed,
In every moment, love is spread.
The beauty grows, a vibrant hue,
In all that represents the true.

Flourishing Together

In the warmth of friendship's light,
We find strength to face the night.
Hand in hand, we rise and fall,
In unity, we conquer all.

Seeds of hope in hearts we plant,
With every heartbeat, dreams chant.
Flourishing like blooms in spring,
Together, we can do anything.

Interlaced Petals

Petals dance on whispered breeze,
Nature's brush paints with such ease.
Colors blend, a sight divine,
In this moment, hearts align.

Interlaced, we find our way,
Guided by the light of day.
In every breath, a story shared,
Together bright, our love declared.

Blossoming Kinship

In the garden of dreams we sow,
Roots intertwined, beginnings flow.
Each petal whispers secrets shared,
In gentle sunlight, love declared.

Together we flourish, side by side,
Embracing the winds, a joyful ride.
With laughter's echo, our hearts align,
In blossoming kinship, forever shine.

Unity in Diversity

Amidst the hues, we stand as one,
A tapestry woven, threads begun.
Cultures blend, like rivers run,
In unity's embrace, we have won.

Differences bloom, with stories vast,
In harmony's dance, shadows cast.
Together we rise, a rainbow's ray,
In diversity's light, we find our way.

Love's Sweet Bouquet

A garden of hearts, fragrant and bright,
Each flower a dream, holding delight.
With petals of kindness, soft and true,
In love's sweet bouquet, I cherish you.

The fragrance of hope, in every breath,
Ties us together, beyond even death.
Through seasons of change, we find our place,
In love's gentle touch, we embrace.

Flourishing Bonds

Roots weave deep in fertile ground,
In trust we gather, love profound.
Each moment nurtured, a sacred tie,
Through storms we weather, reaching high.

With every laugh, our spirits swell,
In shared adventures, tales to tell.
Flourishing bonds, ever so grand,
Together we journey, hand in hand.

United by the Seasons

In springtime's bloom, we find our grace,
Nature awakens, a sweet embrace.
Summer whispers, warm and bright,
Days stretch long, hearts take flight.

Autumn leaves fall, painting gold,
Stories of warmth, forever told.
Winter's chill brings a tender glow,
In every season, love will grow.

The Color of Companionship

In a world of shades, you're my hue,
Together we blend, as colors do.
Every laughter, a vibrant spark,
Painting life bright, banishing dark.

Through shadows cast, we find our way,
In every moment, come what may.
A tapestry woven, with threads of care,
In the canvas of life, we are rare.

The Heart's Garden

Within the heart, a garden grows,
With tender care, each flower knows.
Love is the seed, hope is the rain,
Together we flourish, in joy and pain.

We pull the weeds, and nurture the roots,
In the sun and shade, our spirit shoots.
Every petal speaks of dreams so high,
In this lush haven, we can fly.

Together We Blossom

In the morning light, we stretch our hands,
Reaching for dreams, making our plans.
With roots entwined, we stand so tall,
In each other's strength, we never fall.

When storms arise and shadows loom,
Together we face, dispelling gloom.
Our hearts in sync, a dance divine,
In every moment, together we shine.

Sunshine and Friendship

In morning light, we share a smile,
Through every trial, we walk a mile.
Like beams of sun, we warm the heart,
In laughter's glow, we'll never part.

Together we dance, in joy we soar,
With every hug, we open a door.
In whispered dreams, our secrets bind,
In friendship's light, true love we'll find.

Through stormy skies, we hold each hand,
With hope anew, we take our stand.
Like flowers bloom, so bright and free,
In shades of gold, it's you and me.

In twilight's hush, our stories blend,
Through every season, our hearts extend.
With every sunset, we promise more,
In life's embrace, forever soar.

The Blooming Circle

In gardens green where friendships grow,
A circle formed, with love to show.
Through petals soft, we share our dreams,
In every bloom, a bond redeems.

Each color bright, a tale to tell,
In laughter's sound, our joys do swell.
The earth beneath, with roots entwined,
In every heart, true love aligned.

Through seasons change, we water care,
In gentle hands, a promise rare.
With every spring, new life arrives,
In blooming hearts, our spirit thrives.

In shade of trees, we find our peace,
Where worries fade and joys increase.
With every breeze, our whispers flow,
In friendship's dance, forever grow.

Flourish and Flourish

In quiet moments, seeds are sown,
With tender care, our love has grown.
Through trials faced, we find our way,
In strength united, come what may.

Like rivers flow, our spirits blend,
In harmony, we find our mend.
With every laugh, our spirits soar,
In pushing limits, we seek more.

From tiny sprouts to towering trees,
In every breath, we ride the breeze.
With open hearts, we take the leap,
In every memory, treasures deep.

In twilight's glow, we find our stars,
With dreams in hand, we'll reach afar.
In life's grand tale, together thrive,
In friendship's light, we come alive.

A Symphony of Blooms

In gardens vast, a symphony plays,
With colors bright, and fragrant ways.
Each petal sings a soft refrain,
In nature's choir, we'll rise again.

Through morning dew, our hopes align,
In every breeze, our hearts combine.
With every note, a story shared,
In friendship's song, we are prepared.

From vibrant hues to gentle whites,
In every bloom, a spark ignites.
With every season, new notes arise,
In blooming hearts, the spirit flies.

In harmony, we weave and twine,
With laughter's echo, we brightly shine.
In life's grand opus, we play our part,
In symphonies of blooms, heart to heart.

Together in Grace

In quiet moments, we unite,
Hand in hand, our souls take flight.
Through storms and sun, we find our way,
Together in grace, come what may.

Whispers of hope, like gentle streams,
We nurture each other's dreams.
With love as our guiding light,
We soar, embracing the height.

In laughter and tears, we share our song,
A tapestry of where we belong.
With open hearts, we break each chain,
Together in grace, we rise again.

Shades of Companionship

In the palette of life, we blend,
Each stroke a story, a hand to lend.
With colors bright and shadows deep,
In shades of companionship, we leap.

Moments captured, vivid and true,
In laughter's echo, in skies of blue.
Each hue vibrant, each line a trace,
In the dance of life, we find our place.

With tender brush, we paint our days,
In whispers soft, in joyful praise.
Through changing winds, like leaves in fall,
In shades of companionship, we stand tall.

Faithful Blossoms

In gardens rich, our spirits bloom,
Together we chase away the gloom.
With roots entwined, we share our ground,
Faithful blossoms, love profound.

Through seasons change, our colors thrive,
In harmony, we come alive.
Each petal a promise, each stem a vow,
Faithful blossoms, here and now.

In the warmth of sun, in the rain's embrace,
Steadfast, we grow at a gentle pace.
United we flourish, in joy we trust,
Faithful blossoms, turn to dust.

Collective Joy

In fields of laughter, we run free,
With open hearts, we share our glee.
In every moment, joy we find,
Collective joy, intertwined.

In music's rhythm, our spirits soar,
Like waves on shores, we crave for more.
With each heartbeat, a melody plays,
Collective joy, in endless ways.

Through shared stories, we paint the night,
In the glow of friendship, everything's bright.
Together we rise, hand in hand,
Collective joy, a promised land.

Garden of Common Dreams

In the garden where we meet,
Whispers of hope, soft and sweet.
Petals bloom under sun's gleam,
Together, we nurture our dream.

Paths intertwine, hand in hand,
We cultivate love, understand.
In each corner, memories blend,
Growing together, time we spend.

Beneath the vast and open sky,
Laughter echoes, spirits fly.
In the embrace of gentle trees,
Our hearts dance with every breeze.

Raindrops fall, a soft caress,
Nature's gift we won't suppress.
With each season, we are reborn,
In this garden, dreams are worn.

Colors splash in vibrant hues,
Every shade tells stories true.
In every bloom, a tale resides,
In this haven, love abides.

The Unity of Vibrant Wings

Wings of color, bright and bold,
Stories of courage yet untold.
In the sky, we find our place,
Together we soar, a boundless space.

With every flap, hearts align,
In this flight, our spirits shine.
Navigating through the clouds,
We rise above, breaking crowds.

Harmony sings in the air,
A tapestry woven with care.
Each wingbeat, a thread of peace,
In unity, our fears release.

Tales of struggle we embrace,
In our freedom, we find grace.
Through storms and sun, together we rise,
An orchestra beneath the skies.

Courage blooms in every heart,
No longer alone, never apart.
With vibrant wings, we take the lead,
In this unity, we shall succeed.

Blossoming Bonds of Kinship

Roots entwined beneath the earth,
In our hearts, love finds its birth.
From small seeds, great trees will grow,
In kinship's light, we find our glow.

Moments shared, laughter rings,
In each other, comfort sings.
Through trials faced, we stand as one,
In the shadows, our strength is spun.

Time flows gently, stories weave,
In every memory, we believe.
Through the seasons, bonds will thrive,
In this haven, we are alive.

Hands held tight in the darkest night,
Together we bring forth the light.
With every challenge, bridges form,
A tapestry of warmth in the storm.

In our laughter, joy takes flight,
In the warmth, we know what's right.
Blossoming bonds that never fade,
In kinship's heart, love is made.

Together in a Meadow's Embrace

In the meadow, soft and wide,
With open hearts, we confide.
Flowers bloom in radiant grace,
In this shelter, we find our place.

Breezes whisper tales of old,
In every glance, warmth unfolds.
Through the grasses, laughter flows,
In each moment, love only grows.

Time suspends as sunlight gleams,
Together we weave our dreams.
Underneath the azure dome,
In this embrace, we feel at home.

Birds take flight, a joyful serenade,
In the colors, memories made.
Each step forward, hand in hand,
In this meadow, we understand.

With every heartbeat, we align,
In this beauty, hearts entwine.
Together forever, come what may,
In the meadow's arms, we stay.

Synchronized in the Sun's Warm Glow

Beneath the sun's soft touch, we meet,
Our laughter dances, joy is sweet.
Golden rays weave through the trees,
In this moment, hearts find ease.

Time stands still, a breath we share,
In the warmth, we cast our care.
Echoes of kindness in the light,
Guiding us through day to night.

Together, we are strong and free,
In harmony, just you and me.
The sun teaches us to glow,
In the warmth of love we know.

Shadows lengthen as day fades,
Hand in hand, our joy cascades.
Memories swirl like autumn leaves,
In these moments, our heart believes.

Synchronized, our spirits soar,
In the sun's glow, we want for more.
Every pulse is a shared song,
Together, here is where we belong.

Essence of Shared Seasons

Through vibrant blooms and winter's chill,
We walk the paths, our hearts in thrill.
Spring whispers hope in tender sighs,
While autumn's paintbrush lights the skies.

Summer's laughter fills the air,
Golden moments, we both share.
As seasons change, so do we,
In every shift, we find the key.

Leaves may fall, but roots stay strong,
In answering the life's great song.
Each heartbeat writes a tale anew,
In the essence of me and you.

Gathered moments in twilight's glow,
The world slows down, the stars bestow.
Sharing warmth in the chilly night,
Two souls entwined, in pure delight.

Through every season, we remain,
United under joy and pain.
Forever stitched in time's embrace,
Essence of love, our sacred space.

Colors Merging in the Breeze

A canvas splashed with hues so bright,
Whispers of color, a pure delight.
Petals dance in a gentle flow,
As laughter colors love we sow.

Sky and earth, they intertwine,
In every shade, the stars align.
Rich reds blend with softest blue,
Coloring the world made for two.

Swaying branches, sunlight streams,
Painting pictures built from dreams.
In the breeze, our spirits twirl,
Unfurling tales in this vast swirl.

With every gust, we feel anew,
Together in every hue.
Moments brightened by love's embrace,
Colors merging, our sacred space.

Pulling together, we create,
A masterpiece we celebrate.
In swirling winds, our laughter sings,
Colors mixing, the joy it brings.

The Blooming Caress of Friendship

In a garden where memories grow,
The bloom of friendship starts to show.
Every petal a story to tell,
In fragrant whispers, we both dwell.

Sunlight filters through the leaves,
In each moment, the heart believes.
Roots entwined in shared delight,
Our bond flourishes, ever bright.

Through each season, we nurture care,
In dainty blossoms, we lay bare.
The beauty found in each embrace,
In laughter's glow, we find our place.

Gathered petals in joyful hues,
Every shade reflects what's true.
In summer's warmth or winter's chill,
Our friendship blooms, it always will.

Forever cherished, forever strong,
In the garden where we belong.
With every bloom, our spirits rise,
The caress of friendship never dies.

Echoes in the Garden of Us

In the garden where shadows play,
Whispers of laughter fill the air.
Sunbeams dance on leaves so gay,
Moments captured, memories rare.

The flowers bloom in vibrant hue,
Each petal holds a secret song.
Together we weave dreams anew,
In nature's embrace, we belong.

With every breeze, a story told,
The rustling leaves join in refrain.
Hand in hand, we are bold,
In this garden, joy won't wane.

Beneath the stars, we plant our hopes,
In twilight's glow, hearts entwine.
Together we tread life's slopes,
In this haven, love will shine.

Echoes linger, softly speaking,
A bond that time cannot erase.
In our garden, forever seeking,
A tapestry of warm embrace.

The Dance of Colorful Companionship

In the meadow where wildflowers sway,
Colors burst like laughter's song.
Together we laugh, come what may,
In this dance where hearts belong.

Each petal bright, a friendship's thread,
Twisting gently with the breeze.
We twirl and spin, no words to be said,
In this harmony, we find ease.

The sun dips low, a canvas vast,
Painting memories with a brush of gold.
We cherish these moments, holding fast,
In our hearts, a story unfolds.

Butterflies flutter, on wings so light,
Guiding us through this vibrant scene.
Together we shine, oh, what a sight,
In the dance of life, evergreen.

With each step, a bond we create,
In the rhythm, our spirits soar.
Hand in hand, we celebrate,
Colorful companionship, forevermore.

Unity in Fragrant Layers

In the garden's embrace, scents combine,
Petals whisper secrets, soft and sweet.
Lavender and roses intertwine,
In fragrant layers, we meet.

The air is rich with nature's kiss,
Harmony found in the earth's own grace.
Together we breathe, a moment of bliss,
In this mosaic, time finds its place.

Each layer blooms with stories shared,
Embracing friendships, old and new.
With every blossom, love declared,
In nature's canvas, we renew.

With roots entwined beneath the soil,
We rise together, strong and free.
In unity's embrace, we toil,
Flourishing as one, you and me.

The seasons change, yet still we stay,
In this fragrant world, forever linked.
Together we laugh, together we play,
In unity, our hearts are inked.

Blossoms in Unison

In the dawn's glow, colors awake,
Blossoms stretch, seeking the sun.
In every heartbeat, life we make,
Together, we are forever one.

Nature's orchestra begins to play,
Petals flutter like a soft breeze.
In this moment, come what may,
We find solace beneath the trees.

With vibrant hues, our spirits rise,
In unison, we sing our song.
Amidst the whispers of the skies,
In this harmony, we belong.

The world around us fades away,
As blossoms sway in gentle motion.
In every shade, love finds its way,
In this garden, a shared devotion.

Together we bloom, seasons unfold,
In this sacred place, we thrive.
With every story, a promise told,
Blossoms in unison, we come alive.

Intertwined in Spirit

In whispered winds, we sway and dance,
Memories rich, a timeless trance.
Hearts entwined, forever bold,
In silent vows, our love unfolds.

The stars above, they guide our way,
Through shadowed nights, 'til break of day.
With every breath, our souls ignite,
Together strong, we chase the light.

In stillness found, we share a glance,
A world of dreams, we both romance.
With gentle hands, we weave our fate,
A tapestry, we celebrate.

Through stormy seas, our bond remains,
In laughter's joy, and sorrow's pains.
Each moment shared, a treasure true,
Intertwined spirits, me and you.

With every heartbeat, every sigh,
Our journey flows, as time slips by.
In love's embrace, we find our home,
Together always, we shall roam.

The Garden Path

Amidst the blooms, our laughter rings,
Where sunshine warms, and joy it brings.
Petals soft beneath our feet,
A fragrant world, so pure, so sweet.

Beneath the trees, we pause and dream,
In nature's hush, our hearts redeem.
With every step, our worries fade,
In this oasis, love's serenade.

The colors dance, a vibrant sight,
In harmony, we take delight.
Each flower tells a tale so grand,
Of magic moments, hand in hand.

Through winding paths, our spirits soar,
With whispered hopes, we seek for more.
In nature's arms, our bond we grow,
Together here, forever flow.

As twilight falls, the stars align,
In the garden's heart, your hand in mine.
A symphony that never ends,
On this sweet path, love transcends.

Blooms of Affection

In secret glades, soft blossoms sigh,
With colors bright, they catch the eye.
Each petal holds a whispered wish,
A promise sweet, a tender kiss.

With morning dew, the earth awakens,
In fragrant fields, joy's never shaken.
With gentle hands, we plant our dreams,
In love's embrace, eternal themes.

Through seasons' change, our garden grows,
In every hue, our story flows.
From daffodils to roses fair,
A tapestry of love laid bare.

With every bloom, our hearts connect,
In nature's realm, we find respect.
For every smile, a flower blooms,
Blooming bright within the room.

As twilight falls, we gather near,
In blooms of affection, all is clear.
With every breath, our love ensues,
In nature's beauty, we won't lose.

Hand in Hand

Side by side, we walk the shore,
With every wave, we seek for more.
The tide rolls in, our hearts align,
Hand in hand, your soul with mine.

With every step, the sand we trace,
In laughter's light, we find our place.
Through whispered winds and skies so blue,
A dance of dreams, just me and you.

In twilight's arms, the stars appear,
Together here, there is no fear.
With gentle strength, we face the night,
Hand in hand, we hold on tight.

With every challenge, we stand tall,
In love's embrace, we conquer all.
Through storms we weather, trust expands,
A lifelong journey, hand in hand.

In sunset's glow, our hopes ignite,
With every heartbeat, pure delight.
In this sweet dance, forever grand,
Together always, hand in hand.

Flourish in Sync

In the garden where we grow,
Side by side, we learn to flow.
With gentle hands and open hearts,
Together, each blossom starts.

Under sunlit skies we play,
Dancing softly, come what may.
Every petal holds our dreams,
In harmony, the world redeems.

As seasons change and winds may shift,
Our bond remains a sacred gift.
Through storms and trials, we will stand,
Creating beauty hand in hand.

In twilight's glow, we share our light,
In the silence, we ignite.
A symphony, our hearts will sing,
Finding joy in everything.

From roots entwined, we rise above,
In the dance of life, we move with love.
In every breath, a chance to grow,
Together in this sacred flow.

A Tapestry of Love

Threads of color, intertwined,
Crafting stories, hearts aligned.
In the loom of time we weave,
A tapestry, we both believe.

Each stitch a memory we create,
Binding moments that relate.
With patience, care, and timeless grace,
Our love finds its perfect place.

In the pattern, shades of light,
In every corner, joy takes flight.
Through trials faced and laughter shared,
In this fabric, we are bared.

Knotted threads and gentle seams,
Together, we fulfill our dreams.
As seasons pass, our colors blend,
In this artwork, we transcend.

Our tapestry, a timeless song,
In every note, we both belong.
With every thread, our passion grows,
In this masterpiece, love glows.

Symbiosis of Souls

In a world where hearts connect,
A bond profound we both respect.
Energy flows, a silent guide,
In the depths, our souls abide.

Like rivers merge in gentle streams,
Supporting each other's dreams.
In harmony, we rise and shine,
Two spirits woven, intertwined.

Through every trial, side by side,
In love's embrace, we will confide.
In laughter's echo, in tears that fall,
In this union, we stand tall.

As nature thrives through give and take,
In every moment, we awake.
As seasons shift, we hold the key,
To nurture all that's meant to be.

A cycle pure, we breathe as one,
Through shadowed paths and golden sun.
In life's rich tapestry, we're whole,
In the symbiosis of our soul.

Together We Thrive

Hand in hand, we face the day,
With open hearts, we light the way.
In every challenge, strength we find,
Together, our spirits remind.

As voices rise in joyful song,
A melody where we belong.
With trust as our sturdy foundation,
We dance through life's grand celebration.

In laughter shared, in silence deep,
In promises that we shall keep.
The world is vast, yet here we stand,
Creating dreams with every strand.

Through peaks and valleys, near and far,
You are my light, my guiding star.
In unity, we break the strife,
In every moment, love is life.

Together we thrive, hand in hand,
In this journey, bold we stand.
With every pulse, our hearts entwined,
In this love, true peace we find.

Ties That Bind

In shadowed corners, whispers play,
Threads of friendship weave their way.
Through laughter shared and tears that fall,
Together we rise, united we stand tall.

Time may weather, but bonds remain,
Through stormy nights and summer rain.
In every hug, in every glance,
Love's gentle touch offers a chance.

Distance grows, yet hearts will find,
The strength in arms that won't unwind.
A tapestry of moments shared,
In memories cherished, we are prepared.

From fleeting time, we draw our might,
Each fading dusk, each dawning light.
For in this life, we are entwined,
Forever held by the ties that bind.

Fragrant Embrace

Whispers of petals; sweet perfume,
Nature's touch in every room.
A tender hug from blossoms rare,
In fragrant fields, we lose our care.

Breeze that dances through the trees,
Carries secrets on the breeze.
The sun's warm kiss upon our skin,
In this embrace, we find joy within.

Moments linger, soft and sweet,
Love blooms gently at our feet.
With every scent, our souls entwine,
In fragrant whispers, we define.

In a world of chaos and demand,
We find our peace, hand in hand.
Cocooned in petals, let us be,
Together lost in harmony.

The Garden of Us

In a secret space where dreams take root,
Flowers blossom, their beauty acute.
Each petal tells a tale of hope,
In this garden, together we cope.

Sunlight kisses the leaves so bright,
Dancing shadows play with delight.
Every thorn reminds us too,
That love can hurt, but love is true.

Rain falls softly, washing the ground,
In puddles of joy, our laughter's found.
We plant our dreams, both wild and free,
In this garden, just you and me.

Through seasons change, our roots will stay,
In the garden of us, come what may.
With every bloom, our hearts align,
Together growing, eternally entwined.

Symphony of Colors

A canvas bursts with shades so bright,
Every hue a new delight.
Reds and blues in harmony,
Together they create a melody.

Golden sunbeams, soft and warm,
Gentle whispers that transform.
As twilight falls, the colors blend,
In this symphony, love won't end.

Each stroke guides us through the night,
Illuminated by soft twilight.
In shades of joy, we find our way,
Together painting every day.

Brushstrokes dance like a flowing stream,
In this gallery, we live our dream.
With every splash, our spirits soar,
In this symphony, forever more.

Together We Rise

In shadows deep, we find our light,
Together we stand, ready to fight.
Hand in hand, with hearts so bold,
A tale of courage, we will unfold.

With every step, we climb the hill,
A bond unbroken, shared with will.
Through trials faced, as one we strive,
In unity's strength, together we thrive.

Through storms that rage, we'll hold our ground,
In our voices strong, hope will abound.
As dawn breaks bright, the skies will clear,
The journey ahead, we have no fear.

With every triumph, our spirits soar,
Together in harmony, we'll seek for more.
In laughter shared and tears we shed,
Together we rise, where dreams are led.

A tapestry woven, thread by thread,
In every heartbeat, love's words are spread.
United we journey, side by side,
With faith unshaken, together we ride.

The Language of Bloom

In gardens lush, where flowers sway,
The whispers of petals softly play.
Colors dance on the morning breeze,
A symphony of nature, aiming to please.

Each bloom tells stories, rich and rare,
Of sunlit days and love laid bare.
In every scent, a memory thrives,
The language of bloom, where beauty arrives.

Amidst the greens, a palette bright,
Life's vibrant canvas, pure delight.
From bud to blossom, a tale unfolds,
In silence spoken, in hues so bold.

With bees that hum and birds that sing,
Nature's chorus, a joyful ring.
In every garden, we're all entwined,
The language of bloom, our hearts aligned.

So pause a moment, let nature teach,
In whispered notes, her gifts can reach.
For in each blossom, a lesson lies,
In beauty's language, the spirit flies.

Colorful Union

A spectrum bright, when shades combine,
In every hue, a story line.
Red and blue, in dance they meet,
Creating visions, so blissfully sweet.

With every color, a voice is found,
In vibrant strokes, our hearts are bound.
Together we paint, a world so wide,
In colorful union, we take pride.

Green of the earth, and skies of gray,
Each difference cherished, come what may.
In unity's grasp, we stand in awe,
For love's combination, the perfect law.

From whispered tones to bold displays,
In every blend, our spirit sways.
Together we rise, in joyful spree,
In this colorful union, we are free.

So let us celebrate, with laughter and cheer,
Create a tapestry, year after year.
For in our hearts, and hands held tight,
The art of union, a wondrous sight.

Embracing Nature

In forests deep, where shadows play,
Nature sings in a soft ballet.
Beneath the trees, the whispers flow,
Embracing nature, our spirits glow.

With every breeze that carries leaves,
In rustling echoes, the heart believes.
A symphony of life, pure and free,
In nature's arms, we long to be.

Mountains rise with grandeur high,
Kissing clouds in the endless sky.
In every moment, peace is found,
Embracing nature, our hearts unbound.

The river's song, the ocean's roar,
In every wave, we seek for more.
Together we wander, hand in hand,
In nature's cradle, we make our stand.

So let us cherish this world so green,
In every glimpse, let love be seen.
For in its embrace, we come alive,
In nature's grace, we truly thrive.

The Flowering Connection

In gardens where friendships bloom,
Colors dance, dispelling gloom.
Petals whisper, soft and bright,
Connecting hearts, a joyful sight.

The sun shines down, a golden ray,
Guiding us through each new day.
Roots entwined beneath the ground,
In harmony, we are found.

Each flower tells a tale of past,
Of laughter shared, love unsurpassed.
Through storms and winds, we still stand tall,
Together we rise, never to fall.

In every bloom, a memory lies,
A bond that time will never disguise.
We nurture dreams, both old and new,
In this garden, our friendship grew.

So let us cherish every season,
For in connection, lies the reason.
A tapestry of hearts entwined,
In the flowering connection, we find.

Blossoms of Brotherhood

Beneath the canopy of sky,
We stand as one, we learn to fly.
With every laugh and every tear,
Blossoms of brotherhood draw near.

Branches strong, we hold each other,
In times of need, we are like brothers.
The roots go deep, the bonds grow wide,
In this garden, we take pride.

With every challenge, we will face,
Through sun and rain, we find our place.
The petals shimmer, bright and bold,
In stories of us, together told.

So let us plant these seeds of trust,
In every heart, a bond robust.
With open arms and loving grace,
In our union, find our space.

Together we rise, together we stay,
In blossoms of brotherhood, find our way.
Through every struggle, every win,
In the strength of us, let life begin.

Garden of Dreams

In the garden of dreams we sow,
Hope and visions begin to grow.
With every thought, a seed is cast,
In vibrant colors, futures vast.

The sun drips gold upon the leaves,
Encouraging the heart that believes.
In gentle whispers, dreams take flight,
Guided by the stars' soft light.

Each bloom a wish, a cherished goal,
In the soil of kindness, we find our soul.
Watered by love, nurtured by care,
In this haven, we learn to share.

Through every season, we watch them rise,
With patience, we unveil the skies.
In the garden, we weave our tales,
Through shifting winds and calming gales.

So let us gather, hand in hand,
In this garden, a vibrant land.
With open hearts, we cultivate,
A garden of dreams, we celebrate.

Together in the Sun

Together in the sun we shine,
Our spirits dance, forever entwined.
With laughter loud and hearts so free,
In this warmth, we find our glee.

The rays embrace with gentle touch,
In every moment, we feel so much.
Hand in hand, we walk the path,
In the light, we share our laughs.

With every sunset, we pause to reflect,
On memories made, and paths we select.
Through every trial, we won't retreat,
With love so strong, we feel complete.

Each day a canvas, bright and true,
We paint with colors, bold and new.
Together in the sun, our dreams will soar,
In this journey, we'll always explore.

So let us cherish the light we find,
In every heartbeat, every kind.
Together in the sun, we'll run,
In laughter and love, we are one.

Threads of Affection

In quiet whispers hearts do weave,
The moments shared, the love we cleave.
Through tangled fates, our spirits bind,
In every glance, our joys aligned.

With laughter soft and gentle sighs,
We find our truth in tender ties.
A tapestry of glimmering dreams,
As daylight fades, our passion beams.

The thread pulls tight, each knot a sign,
In every heartbeat, love's design.
With every laugh, our stories meet,
In simple things, our worlds complete.

Through trials faced, our bond stays strong,
In darkest nights, our souls belong.
In warmth of hands, we forge the way,
With hands entwined, come what may.

So let us dance beneath the stars,
With dreams that shine, like endless bars.
In every moment, affection grows,
In threads of love, our journey flows.

The Petal Pathway

Along the way, the petals fall,
A soft embrace, they gently call.
With every step, a fragrant breeze,
In nature's dance, our hearts find ease.

Petals swirl in colors bright,
A pathway lined with pure delight.
With sunlit skies and whispered dreams,
Our souls align like flowing streams.

Beneath the arch of leafy trees,
We wander through the afternoon's ease.
In every bloom, a promise shared,
In every sigh, our hearts laid bare.

The world around us comes alive,
In every petal, hopes will thrive.
With joy as our companion true,
We'll walk this path, just me and you.

And as the twilight paints the sky,
We'll capture moments as they fly.
With petals soft beneath our feet,
Our love will echo, pure and sweet.

Kinship in Full Bloom

In gardens rich with memories,
Our roots entwined, as strong as trees.
With laughter shared, we nurture grace,
In kinship's warmth, we find our place.

Through seasons change, the colors blend,
In every challenge, hand in hand we mend.
Among the blooms, our stories thrive,
In unity, we feel alive.

The petals dance in breezy flight,
In kinship's glow, we find the light.
With every heartbeat, love expands,
A bond that time forever stands.

With open hearts, we greet the dawn,
In every sunrise, we are reborn.
Together we rise, like flowers bold,
In kinship's tale, our lives unfold.

So let us tend this sacred space,
With joy and laughter, grace and grace.
In every bloom, our spirits rise,
In kinship's warmth, forever ties.

A Collective Blossom

In gardens vast, we plant our seeds,
With care and hope, fulfilling needs.
Through hands united, we shall grow,
A collective bloom, love's gentle glow.

Each petal formed from shared embrace,
In unity, we find our place.
A spectrum bright, our colors blend,
In harmony, on dreams we depend.

With every rain, our strength renews,
In every storm, we share our hues.
Through open hearts, we weave the tale,
In every laugh, our spirits sail.

Together we rise, reaching for the sky,
In vibrant echoes, our voices fly.
With roots that run deep, and branches wide,
In this collective bloom, we take pride.

As seasons shift and time moves on,
We'll cherish all the bonds we've drawn.
In this garden of love, forever thrive,
A collective bloom, where dreams arrive.

Bonds Beyond Borders

In whispers of the wind they share,
The laughter flows, transcending air.
A heart in Tokyo beats with pride,
While dreams of Paris flow beside.

From valleys wide to mountains tall,
Every language, a sweet call.
We weave our tales with threads of trust,
In bonds that grow, that always must.

Through oceans vast, love finds a way,
A bridge of hope for every day.
No borders mark what hearts can feel,
Together we create the real.

Through every sunrise, hand in hand,
We dance along this vibrant land.
Though miles may stretch on every side,
Our souls entwined will not divide.

So let us cherish, nurture, grow,
These bonds beyond what we may know.
A tapestry of love so bright,
We steer our dreams towards the light.

The Canvas of Affection

With strokes of love, we paint the day,
In hues of laughter, bright and gay.
Each moment adds a splash of light,
Creating beauty, pure delight.

The canvas swells with every glance,
Where hearts collide, there blooms a chance.
A symphony of colors blend,
As shades of stories gently mend.

In shades of care, the shadows fall,
Each whisper echoes through the hall.
With every brush, our dreams take shape,
A masterpiece the heart does make.

Through trials brushed with pain and tears,
We blend our hopes throughout the years.
In every stroke, affection shows,
A gallery where true love grows.

So let us paint with bold embrace,
The canvas of our sacred space.
In every color, every hue,
We create a world that feels so true.

Blossoms of Belonging

In gardens where the wildflowers sway,
Each petal whispers, here we'll stay.
Together we find strength in roots,
In every thorn, a bond that shoots.

With open hearts, we share our dreams,
In sunlight's glow, our spirit beams.
Through every storm, our courage grows,
In unity, the love just flows.

As seasons change and days drift by,
We stand as trees beneath the sky.
In every leaf and fragrant bloom,
We weave a sense, dispelling gloom.

In laughter's song, through soft embrace,
We find our home in every place.
In every difference, we belong,
Together fierce, forever strong.

So let us nurture what we've sown,
In fields of trust, we've truly grown.
These blossoms bright, they will remain,
A symbol of our joy and pain.

The Union of Greenery

In silken leaves and branches wide,
We find the solace, side by side.
Through dappled light, the laughter flows,
A sanctuary where love grows.

Each fern and flower, a tale to tell,
Of hearts entwined, where we dwell.
In nature's arms, our spirits merge,
As gentle breezes start to surge.

With roots that stretch both deep and strong,
Together, we are where we belong.
In every shade of green, we play,
A vibrant world, where dreams shall stay.

Through seasons turning, ever bold,
In unity, our hearts unfold.
We cherish every leaf and stem,
In this union, we find our gem.

So let us wander, hand in hand,
In the embrace of nature's land.
The union of greenery shall thrive,
Where love and life will always strive.

Whispers of Blooming Hearts

In the garden, secrets play,
Petals dance in soft array.
Colors whisper, sweet and bright,
Gentle breezes take their flight.

Underneath the starlit skies,
Love awakens, softly sighs.
Nature sings a tender tune,
Hearts entwined, like flowers bloom.

Raindrops kiss the thirsty ground,
Joyful laughter all around.
In each moment, joy does spark,
Find the light within the dark.

As the sun begins to rise,
Hope ignites with each surprise.
In this garden, life ignites,
Whispers of hearts, pure delights.

So let love blossom and grow,
Nurtured hearts, a radiant glow.
Together, in this fragrant place,
We find our peace, our warm embrace.

Embrace in Full Blossom

In the shade of leafy trees,
Life unfolds with gentle ease.
Colors burst, a vibrant show,
In the warmth, our spirits flow.

Hands entwined, we stroll along,
Nature's hymn, an endless song.
Petals fall like whispered dreams,
In this realm, our love redeems.

Sunshine weaves through branches wide,
Glistening tears, with joy we bide.
Moments captured, pure and true,
In this bloom, it's me and you.

With each breath, the fragrance lingers,
Telling tales of love that flingers.
Hearts unfurl, like blooms in spring,
Together we embrace this thing.

As shadows lengthen, time goes by,
In this magic, we won't cry.
For each blossom tells the tale,
Of love that's destined to prevail.

Ties of Nature's Tender Touch

In the meadow, where hearts meet,
Nature's touch feels so complete.
Blossoms sway in tender grace,
Each one holds a warm embrace.

Gentle winds bring whispers low,
Secrets that the flowers know.
In the silence, hearts will speak,
Binding love, the strong and weak.

Underneath the moon's soft glow,
Dreams take flight, our spirits flow.
With soft petals as our guide,
In this moment, we confide.

Every fragrance, every sound,
Holds the love that's all around.
Nature's ties, so rich and vast,
In our hearts, forever cast.

So let the blooms remind us well,
Of stories only we can tell.
In this garden, we believe,
In nature's touch, we shall weave.

Threads of Floral Harmony

In the tapestry of blooms,
Life unfolds in vibrant rooms.
Colors weave a tale so bright,
Threads of love in purest light.

Yet the silence speaks aloud,
Nature drapes a gentle shroud.
As the petals start to fall,
We find beauty in it all.

Every whisper, every sigh,
Echoes softly, 'You and I.'
In the garden of our soul,
Love's embrace makes us whole.

So let the flowers teach us grace,
In each delicate, sacred space.
Buds of hope, we watch them soar,
In this harmony, we explore.

As seasons change and petals turn,
In our hearts, the fire will burn.
Threads of floral harmony,
Knit our spirits, wild and free.

Interlocked in Springtime's Grace

In the bloom of tender days,
Buds unfold in soft embrace.
Whispers drift on gentle breeze,
Dancing flowers, hearts at ease.

Sunlight streams through emerald leaves,
Nature's laughter softly weaves.
Every petal, a sweet sigh,
Interlocked beneath the sky.

Colors mix in vibrant hues,
Painting earth with morning dew.
In this symphony of sight,
Joy emerges, pure and bright.

Bees, they hum, a joyful song,
In the fields where we belong.
Springtime's grace, a sweet refrain,
Binding us in love's domain.

Every moment, a shared glance,
In this dance of life, we prance.
Together under skies so blue,
Interlocked, just me and you.

A Symphony of Shared Fragility

In the shadows, softly played,
Fragile hearts in secret laid.
Whispers blend, like falling leaves,
Carrying hopes that never leave.

Through the storms, we walk with grace,
Holding on, an endless chase.
Every glance, a story told,
Shared fragments, gentle and bold.

Fingers touch in silent words,
A symphony of gentle birds.
In the stillness, emotions rise,
Reflections caught in soft sunrise.

With each challenge, shadows sway,
Strength arises, come what may.
Fragile threads that weave and bind,
In our hearts, true love we find.

So let us sing this heartfelt tune,
Under the watchful eye of the moon.
A symphony both strong and sweet,
In our souls, the world's heartbeat.

Harmony in the Floral Tapestry

In fields adorned with colors bright,
Nature hums in pure delight.
Petals fall like gentle rain,
Crafting beauty, easing pain.

Bees and butterflies, a dance,
Life's sweet rhythm, given chance.
Every blossom, a song to sing,
Harmony that spring will bring.

Sunrise paints the morning glow,
Nature's art in ebb and flow.
Each flower tells a whispered tale,
In this tapestry, we prevail.

With gentle hands, we weave hope,
Creating bonds through every scope.
Harmony resides in every shade,
In the love and life we've made.

Entwined in roots, we grow as one,
Underneath the warming sun.
In this garden, we shall thrive,
Floral tapestry, alive.

Nature's Kindred Spirits

In the quiet, we can feel,
Nature's pulse, a sacred seal.
Every rustle, every breeze,
Whispers soft among the trees.

Birds in chorus, rising high,
Echoes sweet against the sky.
In the stillness, hearts unite,
Guided by a shared delight.

Waves that crash upon the shore,
Remind us what we're longing for.
Every moment, tender grace,
Nature's arms, our warmest place.

Stars above, a twinkling thread,
Connecting dreams in dreams we've fed.
Kindred spirits, hand in hand,
Together in this wondrous land.

Through the seasons, ebb and flow,
In this bond, we're free to grow.
Nature's heart beats close to ours,
In her beauty, life empowers.

Harmony in Bloom

The sun rises soft and bright,
Petals open to greet the light.
Colors blend in sweet embrace,
Nature sings in gentle grace.

Whispers of the morning breeze,
Fluttering through the blooming trees.
Every note a perfect tune,
A promise shared beneath the moon.

Birds take flight, a joyful sound,
In this vibrant space, peace is found.
Life's a dance, free and bold,
Each day a story waiting to be told.

With every budding bloom we see,
Harmony flows endlessly.
Together, we find our way,
In the warmth of every day.

Through gardens lush, we wander far,
Guided by a shining star.
Each petal a moment shared,
In harmony, we all are paired.

Interwoven Hearts

In a tapestry of dreams we weave,
Threads of love we dare to believe.
Hearts entwined in gentle sway,
Together facing each new day.

Whispers echo through the night,
In shadows cast, we find our light.
Every glance a spark of fire,
Filling souls with deep desire.

Moments captured, sweet and rare,
In the stillness, we lay bare.
Hands held tight, we face the storm,
Finding shelter in each arm.

With every heartbeat, time unfolds,
Stories of love yet to be told.
Two souls dance in synchrony,
Interwoven beautifully.

The world fades, just you and me,
In this bond, we find the key.
Through every challenge, we will rise,
Together, we will touch the skies.

Garden of Kindred Spirits

In the garden of vibrant souls,
Where laughter echoes, love consoles.
Kindred spirits gather near,
In this haven, all is clear.

Each flower blooms with stories shared,
In every petal, hope is bared.
Connection flows through roots so deep,
In this space, all dreams we keep.

With gentle hands, we tend the earth,
Celebrating each spirit's worth.
In unity, we start to grow,
Together, we ebb and flow.

The sun will rise, the moon will glow,
In this garden, love will flow.
Every moment a cherished gift,
Kindred hearts, forever adrift.

Here, we nurture, here we thrive,
In this garden, we come alive.
A sanctuary where dreams align,
Together, we eternally shine.

Dance of the Flowers

In the meadow, flowers sway,
Dancing joyfully each day.
Colors twirl beneath the sky,
Nature's rhythm floating by.

Gentle breezes, whispers soft,
Lift the petals, ever aloft.
Ballet of blooms, a grand display,
Each moment begs us to play.

The sun shines bright on vibrant hues,
In this ballet, we find our muse.
Every flower tells a tale,
In the wind, we hear the gale.

With graceful steps, they twine and bend,
In the dance that will not end.
Nature's beauty all around,
In this harmony, joy is found.

Let us join this dance so free,
Flow with nature's melody.
Together, we twirl and spin,
In the dance of life, we win.

Sprouts of Collective Joy

In gardens wide, we plant our dreams,
Shared laughter dances in sunlit beams.
Together we water hopes that grow,
In the warmth of friendship, love will flow.

With each sprout, a new story unfolds,
In the tapestry of life, joy beholds.
United we stand, hand in hand we strive,
In the heart of the garden, we come alive.

The petals unfurl, colors collide,
In the symphony of life, we take pride.
With roots intertwined, our spirits entwined,
In this fertile soil, bliss we find.

Through rains and storms, we remain aligned,
In the embrace of hope, our dreams defined.
From each budding flower, we glean delight,
In the light of togetherness, we take flight.

So let's nurture this bond, wild and free,
In every season, you'll bloom with me.
Together we rise, together we grow,
In the garden of joy, let the love flow.

In Harmony with Nature's Gift

Beneath the boughs where whispers play,
Nature sings in wondrous array.
The breeze carries tales of times gone by,
As echoes of earth blend with the sky.

In the rustle of leaves, a secret shared,
In each drop of dew, a moment spared.
With the sun's warm kiss, our spirits soar,
In harmony with nature, we seek more.

Mountains stand tall, rivers flow wide,
In the heart of the wild, we take pride.
Together with wildlife, we intertwine,
In the dance of existence, our souls align.

The flowers bloom, painting the land,
In a blend of colors, a master's hand.
With each gentle breeze, a hymn we sing,
In the cradle of nature, we find spring.

We walk hand in hand, as one with the earth,
In every heartbeat, we feel its worth.
In this boundless garden, endless and free,
We honor our home, in unity we be.

Weaving Together Floral Dreams

In the garden of thoughts, we sow our seeds,
With petals of hope and vibrant deeds.
Weave the fabric of life with care,
In every stitch, our dreams we share.

With colors bright, we create our art,
In the tapestry of love, each plays a part.
Together we blossom, side by side,
In this floral embrace, let joy abide.

The fragrant blooms whisper stories old,
With the warmth of friendship, courage bold.
In the gentle breeze, our wishes take flight,
In the canvas of day, we merge light.

As petals unfold, our visions align,
In the melody of growth, souls entwine.
Through thorns and shadows, we journey on,
In the garden we've nurtured, hope is reborn.

So let's gather blooms, our dreams in a vase,
With heads held high, we embrace each space.
In the art of togetherness, we will thrive,
In the heart of the garden, we come alive.

Concord of the Blooming Heartstrings

In the quiet whispers of the dawning light,
Hearts intertwine, lifting spirits bright.
With every bloom, connections deepen,
In the garden of souls, love is the beacon.

The vibrant colors call to the wise,
Beneath the vast canvas of skies.
Together we flourish, united in song,
In the rhythm of nature, we belong.

With petals of kindness, we craft our way,
In the dance of the blossoms, we celebrate play.
Every heart a note in the symphony grand,
In the chorus of life, we take a stand.

The fragrance of unity fills the air,
In every heartbeat, we find care.
With each gentle breeze, stories unfold,
In the embrace of love, warmth we hold.

So let us gather, hearts open wide,
In this garden of love, together we bide.
In the concord of blooms, our spirits will rise,
In the beauty of togetherness, we find skies.

A Circle of Color

In the meadow bright and bold,
A tapestry of hues unfold,
Blossoms dance in gentle breeze,
Whispers found among the trees.

Petals soft in morning light,
Paint the world in pure delight,
Every shade tells its own tale,
Together, they will never pale.

Crimson, blue, and gold entwined,
Nature's heart, a gem defined,
Each a part of the grand scene,
Bound together, evergreen.

Rainbow arcs through summer's day,
Inviting all to come and play,
A vivid bond, a sweet embrace,
In this circle, find our place.

As daylight fades to dusky gray,
Colors linger, softly sway,
In memory, they softly bloom,
A circle framed in nature's room.

Symbiosis in Nature

In the forest, life entwines,
All connected, like the vines,
Roots beneath the soil's seam,
Nature's ever-flowing dream.

Birds and bees in harmony,
Flowers bloom so tenderly,
Each small part a vital role,
Together, they make one whole.

Creeks and stones in sweet embrace,
Share their journeys in this space,
Fish and frogs, a song they share,
In rhythms soft, a silent prayer.

Clouds above and earth below,
Wind that stirs the leaves to flow,
In this dance, we learn and grow,
A symbiosis we all know.

Every sound, a breath of life,
Harmony in day and strife,
Nature teaches, pure and clear,
In symbiosis, hold us near.

The Garden of Kinship

In a garden, hand in hand,
Together we will make a stand,
Seeds of trust in soil so deep,
Bonding roots that we will keep.

Sunlight warms our hopeful hearts,
Nurtured dreams, a world that starts,
As flowers bloom, our spirits rise,
Reflecting love that never dies.

With every leaf, a story shared,
Moments cherished, love declared,
In laughter's breeze, we find our way,
In unity, we stand and play.

Come gather 'round, find your place,
In this garden, seek your grace,
Petals fall like whispered vows,
In kinship, may we find our hows.

From tiny seeds to mighty trees,
In this space, we share the ease,
The garden thrives, a bond so true,
In kinship's light, forever new.

Collective Garden

In the heart of every town,
Lies a garden, roots go down,
Hands come together, rich and free,
Planting hopes for all to see.

Colors bursting, life at play,
A collective that greets the day,
Voices rise in unity,
Celebrating diversity.

Underneath the shared blue sky,
We find strength, we dare to fly,
As blossoms bloom, we take a stand,
In this garden, hand in hand.

Harvests gathered, joy abounds,
In every heart, a love resounds,
Together cultivating dreams,
In collective, our spirit gleams.

As seasons change and time flows on,
We tend these roots, though leaves are gone,
In this garden, we will thrive,
A tapestry of hearts alive.

Whispers of Unity

In the quiet night, we find our song,
Voices unite where we all belong.
Hands touch gently, a warmth we share,
In whispers of love, we're always there.

Through trials faced, we stand as one,
Under the sky, where dreams are spun.
Together we rise, never alone,
In whispers of hope, our hearts have grown.

Beneath starlit skies, our spirits soar,
Each step together, we open the door.
With laughter and tears, the journey's bright,
In whispers of unity, we find our light.

In every heartbeat, a rhythm flows,
Connected in purpose, as friendship glows.
With open minds, we break the chains,
In whispers of unity, love remains.

As dawn breaks softly, we greet the day,
With dreams in our eyes, we find our way.
In the tapestry woven, our stories blend,
In whispers of unity, joy will never end.

Blooms in Harmony

In gardens bright, where flowers bloom,
Colors dance in sweet perfume.
Petals whisper to the breeze,
In harmony, they find their ease.

A symphony of hues so bold,
Stories of love and life unfold.
Together they sway, a vibrant show,
In blooms of harmony, hearts will grow.

Sunshine kisses each tender leaf,
Growing through joy, through moments brief.
In the quiet earth, their roots entwine,
In blooms of harmony, life does shine.

As seasons change, they stand so tall,
Through storm and sun, they'll never fall.
Each bloom a promise, a song so sweet,
In blooms of harmony, we feel complete.

With every bud, new dreams arise,
Together they paint the endless skies.
In nature's garden, let love sing free,
In blooms of harmony, we become we.

Threads of Shared Dreams

In twilight's glow, our visions weave,
Threads of dreams that we believe.
Each stitch a story, a path we chart,
In shared dreams, we find our heart.

Through valleys low, and mountains high,
With every laugh, we touch the sky.
Together we craft what we aspire,
In threads of dreams, we build our fire.

With every heartbeat, we find our way,
Guided by hope, come what may.
In the fabric of life, our spirits dance,
In threads of shared dreams, we take our chance.

As colors merge, a canvas bright,
Together we paint our shared delight.
In each gentle moment, our stories blend,
In threads of shared dreams, love transcends.

With eyes on the stars, we boldly steer,
In the journey of life, we hold you near.
In every whisper of the night, we gleam,
In threads of shared dreams, we live the dream.

Blossoms of Connection

In the garden of time, we plant our seeds,
Watered by kindness, love is what feeds.
Roots intertwine, in soil so rich,
In blossoms of connection, we find our niche.

As seasons shift and colors change,
Through every struggle, we rearrange.
With hands united, we grow and thrive,
In blossoms of connection, we come alive.

Each bloom a memory, tender and bright,
Together we stand, face the night.
In fragrant whispers, our souls take flight,
In blossoms of connection, we shine so bright.

Through gentle breezes, our laughter flows,
In every heart, a garden grows.
Celebrating life with every breath,
In blossoms of connection, we conquer death.

With open hearts, we journey far,
In the tapestry of life, you are our star.
In every moment, bright and true,
In blossoms of connection, we bloom anew.

Collective Bloom

In gardens where we gather,
Petals dance in the light,
Colors blend with laughter,
Nature whispers, pure delight.

Together we plant our dreams,
Hope sprouting every day,
Hearts entwined in sunbeams,
As we watch the shadows play.

With hands dirtied by the earth,
We nurture what we sow,
Each flower tells our story,
In this space, love will grow.

Season's change, we stand tall,
Roots embrace the soil wide,
Through the storms, we will call,
In each other, we confide.

Together, we bloom as one,
In harmony we rise,
Underneath the warming sun,
Our spirits touch the skies.

Scented Memories

In fields where roses linger,
Fragrances weave through the air,
Whispers of distant summers,
Time captured, woven with care.

Breezes carry soft perfume,
Echoes of laughter and light,
Each scent a brush with life,
Guiding hearts through the night.

Memories dance like shadows,
In gardens of yesteryear,
With every bloom that blossoms,
We find all that we hold dear.

Fragrance wraps around us tight,
Reminding us of the past,
In each note, a gentle sigh,
A love that was meant to last.

Through the seasons, we remember,
Scented trails of the sweet,
Holding on to the warmth, dear,
In our hearts, they remain meet.

The Ties We Cultivate

Beneath the softest twilight,
We share our dreams and fears,
Each word a thread of trust,
Woven through the passing years.

In fields of open futures,
We sow a bond so true,
With every seed we scatter,
Together, me and you.

The roots that intertwine us,
In soil rich with love's grace,
Through sunshine and through rain,
We find our sacred place.

With every gentle gesture,
The ties grow ever strong,
In laughter and in silence,
We write our lasting song.

Cultivating our spirit,
With patience and with care,
In this garden we flourish,
Every moment, we share.

United in Nature

Underneath the vast sky,
Where horizons freely meet,
We find the peace of nature,
In every wild retreat.

Mountains stand in silence,
Rivers run with gentle grace,
In the embrace of wilderness,
We discover our own place.

Birds sing to greet the morning,
As leaves dance with the breeze,
In the heart of the forest,
We breathe in, and we seize.

Connected to each moment,
In harmony we tread,
Nature's voice, our anthem,
In every path we're led.

Together, we are stronger,
In unity we thrive,
With nature as our canvas,
In this world, we come alive.

Nurtured by the Breeze

Whispers of wind, soft and sweet,
Carrying dreams on nimble feet.
Through the trees and fields it glides,
In nature's arms, the spirit rides.

Gentle caress, a lover's sigh,
Lifting hopes to meet the sky.
With every breath, life starts anew,
In the dance of leaves, so true.

Kisses of sun, warm and bright,
Chasing shadows, bringing light.
The world awakens, heart aligned,
Embraced by nature, love defined.

In the stillness, moments bloom,
Casting away the veil of gloom.
Nurtured hearts find comfort there,
Wrapped in silence, soft as air.

A Haven of Colors

In gardens where the petals play,
Colors mingle in bright array.
Birds sing sweetly, skies so wide,
A symphony where dreams abide.

Lilies white and roses red,
Dancing thoughts in petals spread.
Golden rays that beckon light,
Nature's canvas, pure delight.

Harmony in every hue,
Painted whispers, soft and true.
Each blossom a tale to share,
A haven found in fragrant air.

In the stillness, time stands still,
Brush of nature, gentle thrill.
Life's beauty in full view,
A promise made in colors new.

Hearts in Bloom

Underneath the evening sky,
Hearts awaken, softly sigh.
In the meadow, love unfolds,
A treasure trove of stories told.

Petals brush against the soul,
Whispers of the heart's sweet goal.
With each dawn, a new refrain,
Life's bright canvas, love's domain.

Hands entwined in gentle grace,
Finding warmth in each embrace.
In the fragrance, hopes arise,
Two hearts dance beneath the skies.

Time moves slowly, moments glide,
In this haven, love's sweet tide.
A world where dreams take flight,
Hearts in bloom, a pure delight.

The Wildflowers' Embrace

Wildflowers sway in summer's breeze,
Painting hills with vibrant ease.
Each bloom tells a tale so bright,
Dancing freely, pure delight.

Amidst the grass, a secret shared,
Nature's beauty, unprepared.
In every color, stories weave,
A tapestry that we believe.

Butterflies flit, a joyful play,
In the sun's warm, golden ray.
Life's sweet chaos, a perfect blend,
Wildflowers bloom, love's true friend.

Hearts uplifted, spirits soar,
In the embrace of nature's core.
Whispers of wind, softly call,
In wildflowers, we find it all.

www.ingramcontent.com/pod-product-compliance
Ingram Content Group UK Ltd.
Pitfield, Milton Keynes, MK11 3LW, UK
UKHW021524280125
4335UKWH00036B/985